WOMEN WHO DOMINATED IN SPORTS

Sports Book Age 6-8
Children's Sports & Outdoors Books

Speedy Publishing LLC
40 E. Main St. #1156
Newark, DE 19711
www.speedypublishing.com
Copyright 2017

All Rights reserved. No part of this book may be reproduced or used in any way or form or by any means whether electronic or mechanical, this means that you cannot record or photocopy any material ideas or tips that are provided in this book.

For a long time, women's sports was in the background, and male athletes got all the support and all the fame. That has changed! Here are some great women athletes to admire!

TENNIS

MARTINA NAVRATILOVA

Navratilova, from the Czech Republic, was almost unbeatable. Between 1982 and 1996 she won 428 singles matches out of 442. In 1983 she won 86 matches and lost only one! In 1984 she was part of a doubles team with Pam Shriver that won 109 matches in a row.

Serena Williams

SERENA WILLIAMS

Williams, from California, started her career as "the sister of Venus Williams". But she is now considered one of the best tennis players of all time. She was won more than 35 Grand Slam titles and four Olympic tennis medals. In the process she has remade the image of women tennis players: her grace and good behavior toward others are a model for all young players.

MARGARET COURT

Margaret Court was a top-ranked women's tennis player. During her career she won over 90 percent of her tournaments on all surfaces—hard, clay, grass, and carpet courts. She won more tennis titles than any other player.

Gymnastics

OLYMPICS

NADIA COMANECI

Comaneci, from Romania, was the first woman ever to win a perfect "10" score in an Olympic gymnastics event. Over her career, she won more than 20 gold medals, including five in various Olympic events. Her perfect score of 10 on the uneven bars in the 1976 Olympics was so unexpected that the scoreboard was not even able to display it. The manufacturer had been told that nobody could ever score a 10! The scoreboard had to show "1.00" instead.

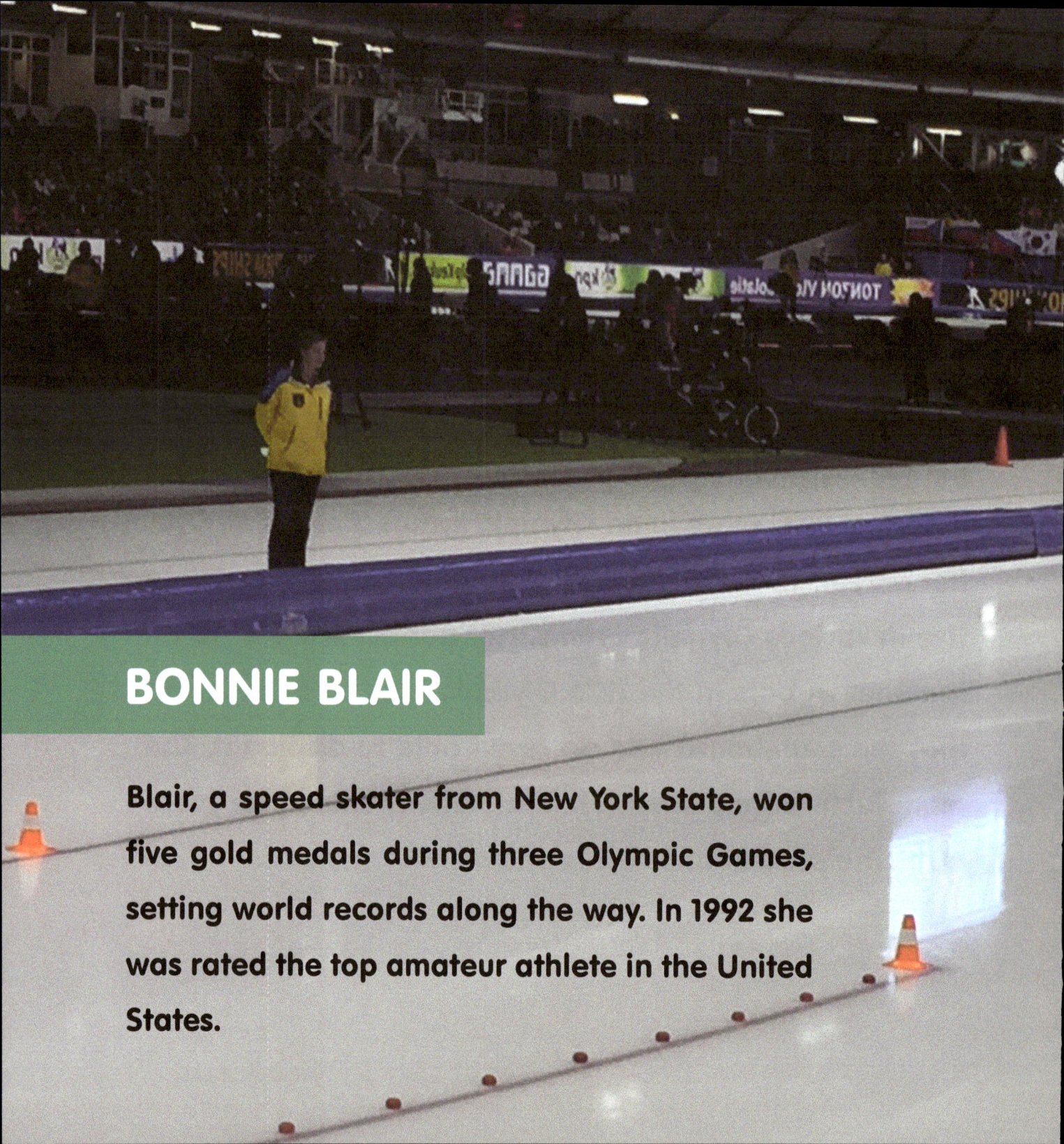

BONNIE BLAIR

Blair, a speed skater from New York State, won five gold medals during three Olympic Games, setting world records along the way. In 1992 she was rated the top amateur athlete in the United States.

Track and Field Stadium

FLORENCE GRIFFITH JOYNER

This runner, nicknamed "Flo-Jo", set speed records for the 100 and 200 meter sprints in 1988 that nobody else has come close to breaking. She was so fast on the track that officials tested her many times to see if she was using performance-enhancing drugs. Every time the tests reported that she was using no such substances.

Equestrian

ANKY VAN GRUNSVEN

Anky van Grunsven, from the Netherlands, is a champion equestrian (horseback rider). She has won more Olympic medals than any other equestrian, including three medals in a row in the same event in three different Olympic Games.

Fanny Blankers-Koen

FANNY BLANKERS-KOEN

Francina Blankers-Koen, a Dutch athlete, won four gold medals at the 1948 Olympic Games. At the time she was thirty years old and the mother of two children. In those days, people did not think mothers could accomplished very much in competition, and her nickname was "The Flying Housewife". Starting in 1935, Blankers-Koen set world records in long jump, high jump, hurdling, and sprint. She won almost 60 Dutch and five European championships, and set twelve world records in a variety of sports. She was voted Female Athlete of the Century in 1999.

BETTY CUTHBERT

Cuthbert is an Australian runner who won four Olympic gold medals. With her distinctive running style, with a high knee lift, Cuthbert has set world records at distances ranging from 60 meters to 440 yards.

Statue of Betty Cuthbert

Rhythmic Gymnastics

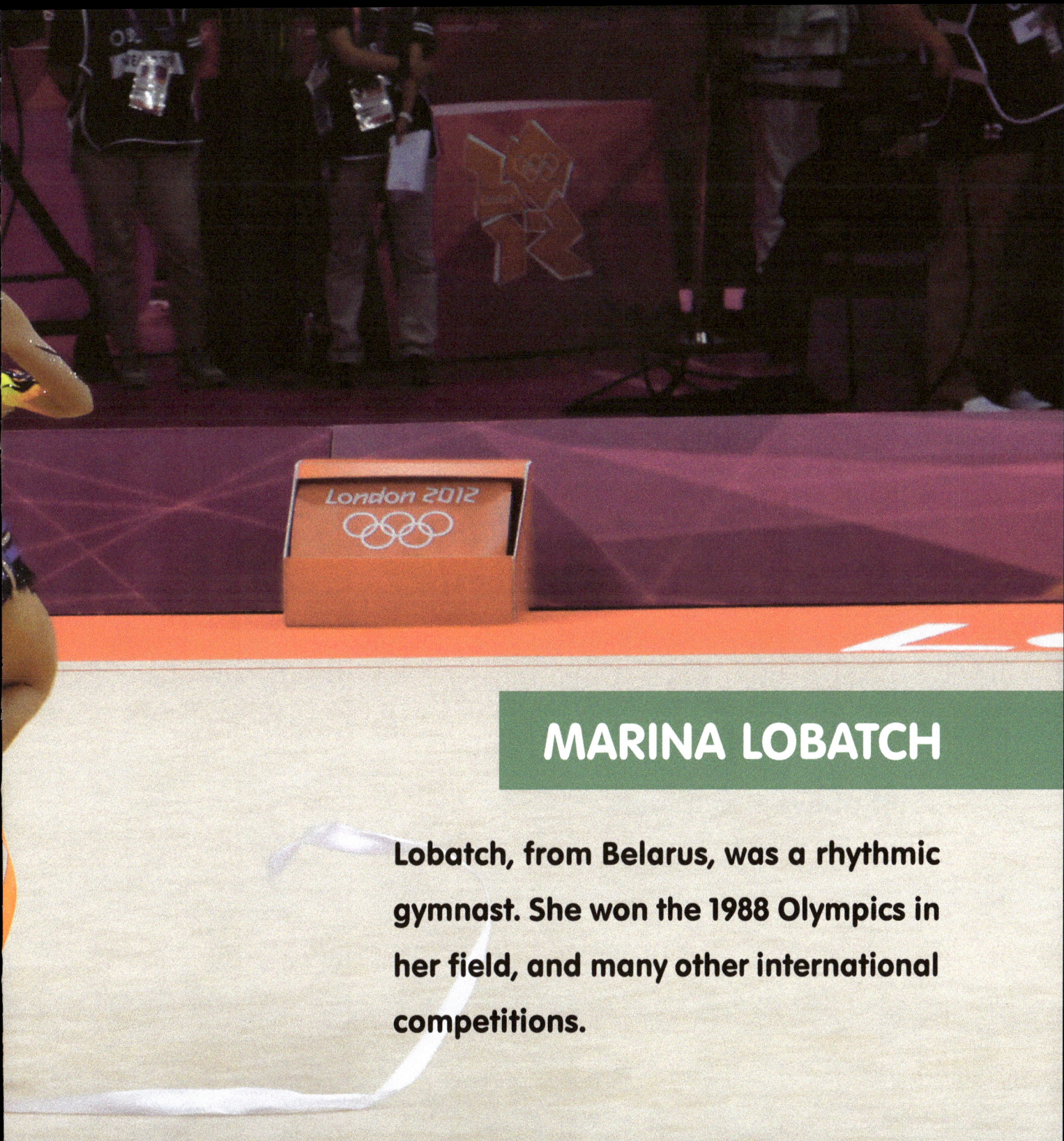

MARINA LOBATCH

Lobatch, from Belarus, was a rhythmic gymnast. She won the 1988 Olympics in her field, and many other international competitions.

YELENA ISINBAYEVA

Yelena Gadzhievna Isinbayeva, from Russia, was considered the best female pole-vaulter in history. She won Olympic gold medals twice, and was the first woman to pole-vault above five meters.

Pole Vault

Gymnastics

LARISA LATYNINA

Larisa Latynina was a gymnast representing the Soviet Union. She won 14 individual gold medals, and four team medals, at the Olympic Games between 1956 and 1964. She helped establish the Soviet Union as a world power in gymnastics.

SONJA HENIE

Sonja Henie, from Norway, won three Olympic gold medals in figure skating, was European champion six times, and was world champion ten times. In all, she won more major titles in her sport than any other ladies' figure skater. After she retired from sports she became a leading movie star in Hollywood.

WOMEN'S BASKETBALL

LYNETTE WOODARD

Woodward, a United States athlete, was so good at college, amateur, Olympic, and professional basketball from the 1970s into the 1990s that many of her career records (such as points scored and rebounds) still stand. She played college basketball from 1977 to 1981, but was still selected to play in the women's professional league, the WNBA, over twenty years later, in 1997. She was captain of the U.S. women's basketball team that won the gold medal at the 1984 Olympics. The following year she became the first-ever female member of the famous Harlem Globetrotters team.

MIA HAMM

Hamm played soccer for the United States for 17 seasons, and was World Player of the Year twice. She was an incredible player, both for her abilities on the field and for her work to popularize women's soccer as a serious sport. Many young women took up the game after seeing Hamm play.

SOCCER

Marianne Vos

CYCLING

MARIANNE VOS

Vos is a Dutch cyclist who is often considered one of the best in bicycle racing of all time, either male or female. She became the champion at road-racing and cyclo-cross at 19 years old. She has won several Olympic gold medals and has won the world road race championship three times.

MULTI-SPORT ATHLETES

JACKIE JOYNER-KERSEE

Kersee, of the United States, won medals at four different Olympic Games in heptathlon and long jump, and won further medals at other international competitions like the Pan American Games. She was also a remarkable basketball player. She was a starter for four college seasons as well as playing professionally after the end of her Olympic career.

Heptathlon

Zaharias Museum

BABE DIDRIKSON ZAHARIAS

Zaharias, at five feet, seven inches and 115 pounds, was not large or dominating. But she seemed to be very good at every sport she tried. She was an All-American basketball player, won medals in three different events (javelin, 80-meter hurdles and high jump) at the 1932 Olympic Games, and then became one of the best golfers of all time. She won over 40 professional golf tournaments. She even pitched an inning in a men's professional baseball game! She was diagnosed with cancer, but continued competing until her death at the age of 45.

CAROLINA KLÜFT

Carolina Evelyn Klüft was a Swedish athlete. She was a champion in many track-and-field events, including triple jump, long jump, heptathlon, and pentathlon. As well as winning world and European championships several times, she won an Olympic gold medal in heptathlon in 2004. Starting in 2002, she won 22 consecutive heptathlon and pentathlon competitions.

Long Jump

SWIMMING

KATIE LEDECKY

Ledecky, of the United States, won five gold medals and set three world records when she competed in the 2015 swimming world championships at the age of 18. She has so far won six Olympic medals and awards in many other international competitions.

LINDSEY VONN

U.S. skier Lindsey Vonn has won four World Cup skiing championships, and won two Olympic medals. She has won more downhill skiing and Super G competitions than any other female skier.

SKIING

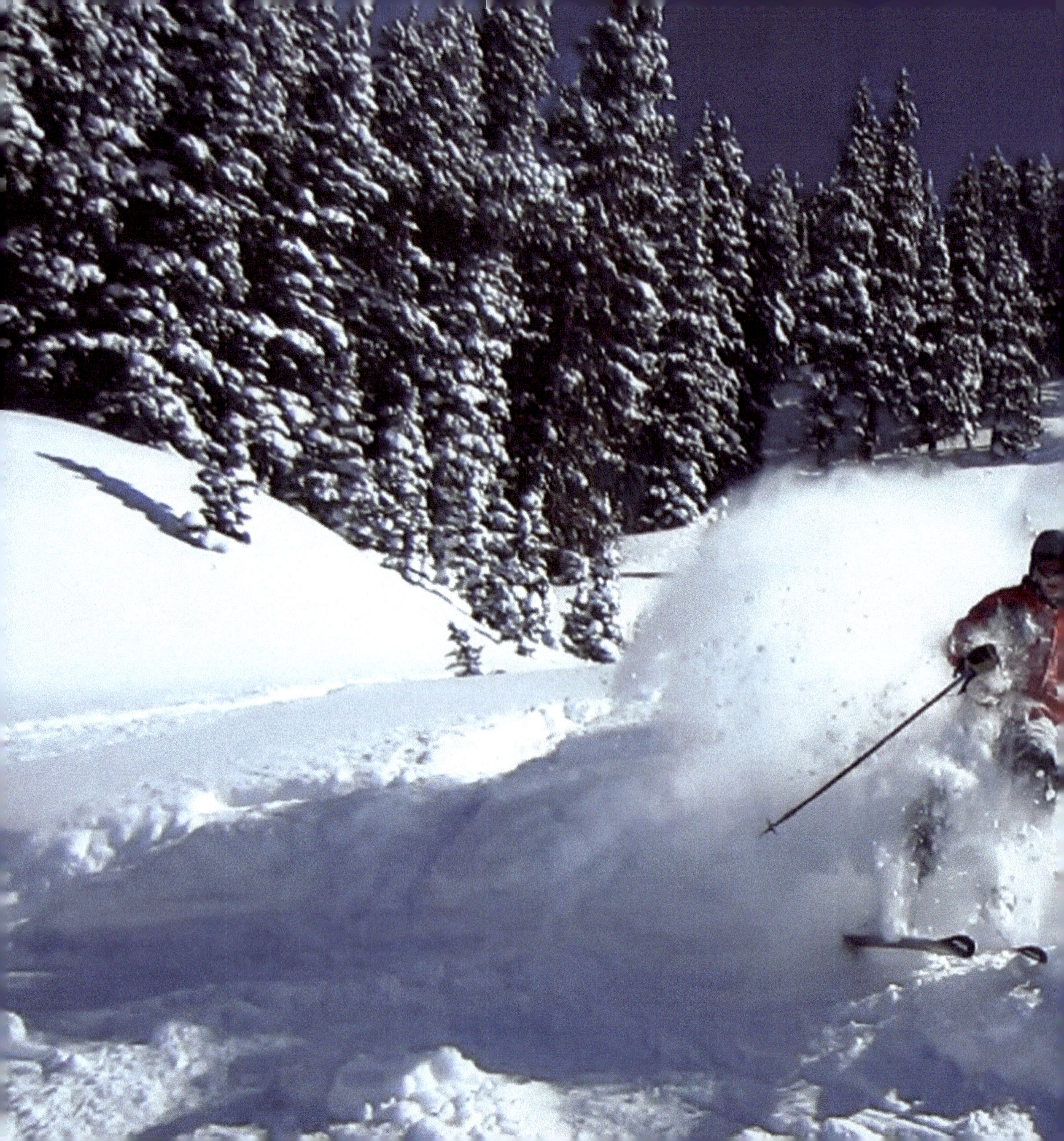

JANICA KOSTELIĆ

Kostelić, from Croatia, was a dominant alpine skier. She won Olympic medals four times, as well as five gold medals at the skiing world championships.

TINA MAZE

Maze, from Slovenia, is one of her country's most successful Olympic athletes. She won two gold medals at the 2014 Winter Olympics. She was named Slovenia's female athlete of the year five times between 2005 and 2014.

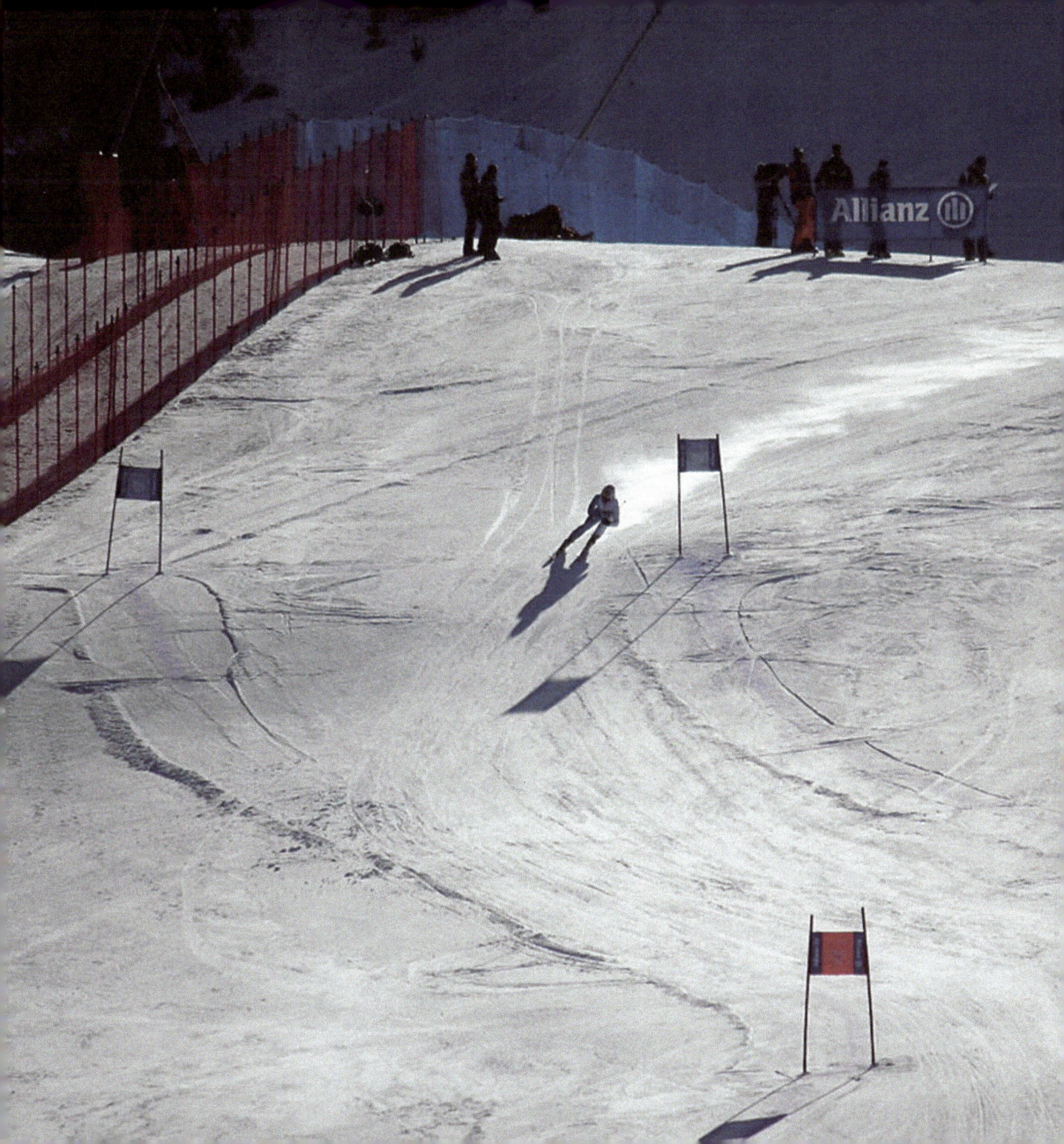
Allianz

Marit Bjørgen

MARIT BJØRGEN

Bjørgen is from Norway, and was a champion cross-country skier. She won over 100 competition victories in her career in cross-country skiing, and almost 30 victories in sprint competitions. She was the top medal-winner at the 2010 Winter Olympics, and three of her five medals were. She won three more gold medals at the Winter Olympics in 2014.

RUNNING

EDNA KIPLAGAT

Edna Ngeringwony Kiplagat is a long-distance runner from Kenya. She has won marathons in competitions all over the world. A marathon is a race of over twenty-six miles, and Kiplagat's personal record for that distance is under two hours and twenty minutes.

Marathon Runners

Paula Radcliffe

PAULA RADCLIFFE

Radcliffe, from England, was a remarkable long-distance runner. She won the London and New York marathons three times each. She set the women's marathon world record in 2002, and as of this writing her speed record has not been broken. Radcliffe took part in the Olympics four times between 1996 and 2008, and has won or received medals in many international tournaments.

GOLF

ANNIKA SORENSTAM

Sorenstam, from Sweden, had one of the most successful professional golf careers in history. She won more than 90 international tournaments, and was named Player of the Year eight times.

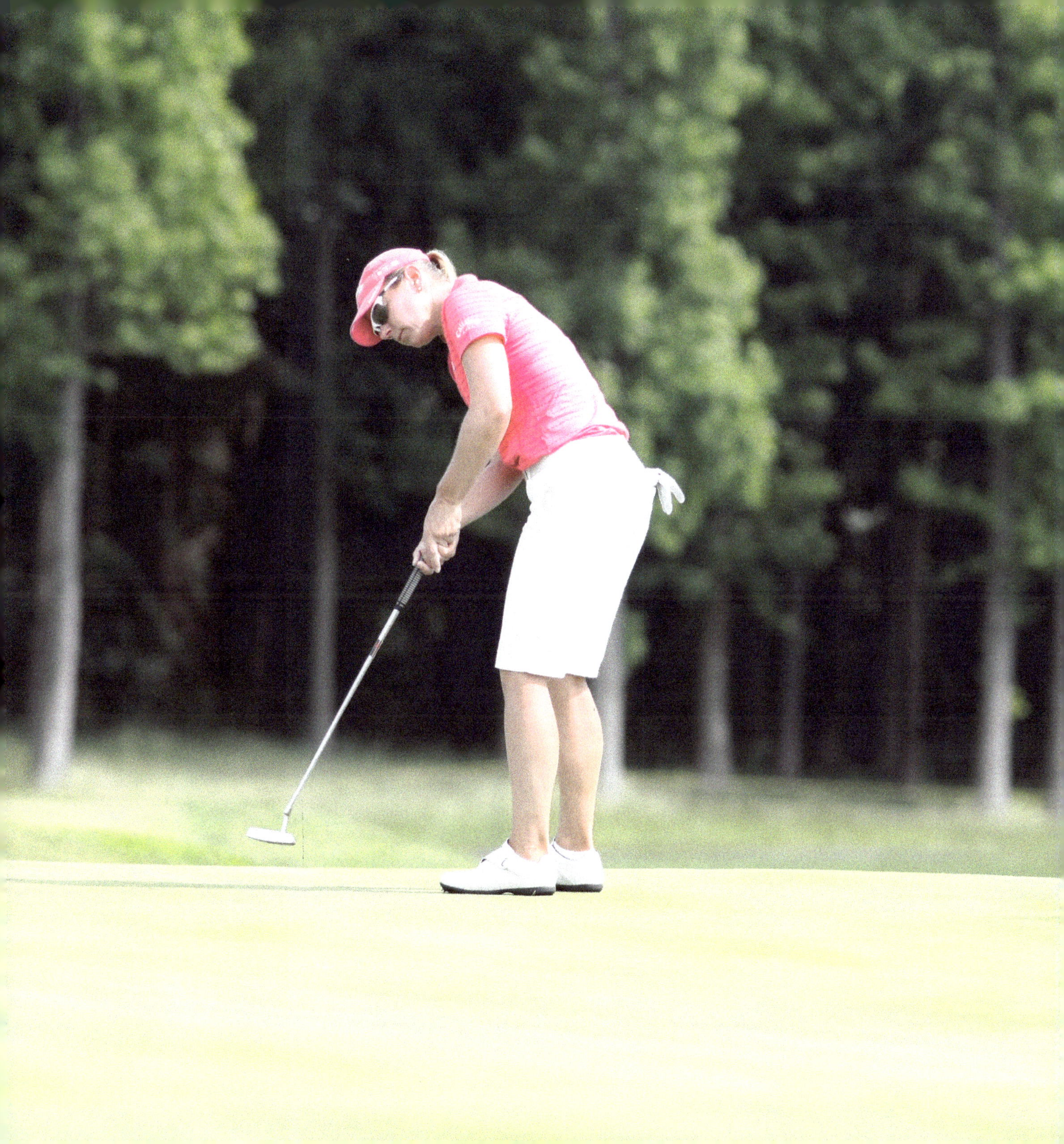

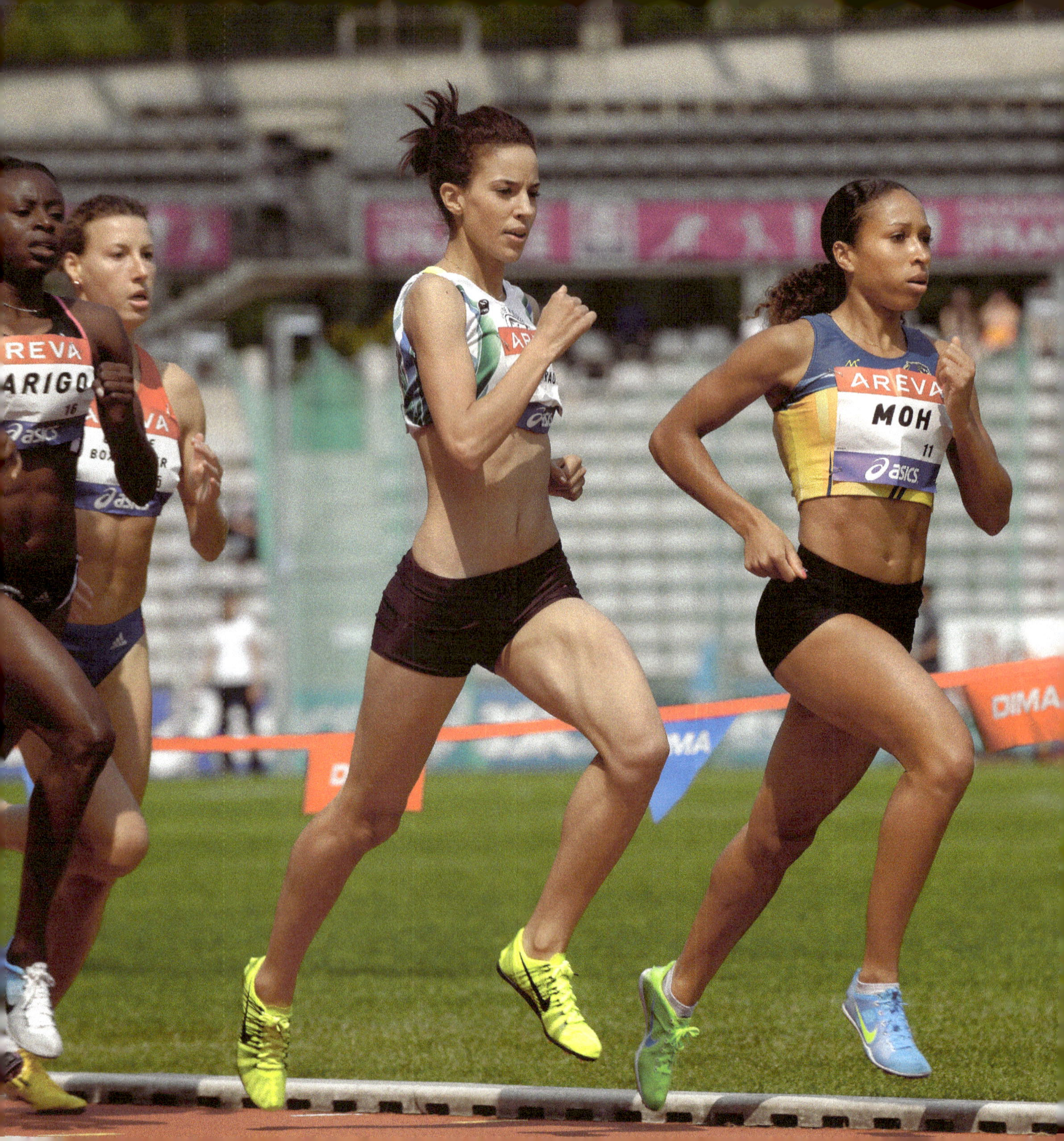
AREVA
MOH
11
asics
AREVA
ARIGO
16
asics
DIMA

REMARKABLE WOMEN

All these women accomplished remarkable things in their fields, many of them at a time when the world considered women as second-rate and less worthy of attention than men.

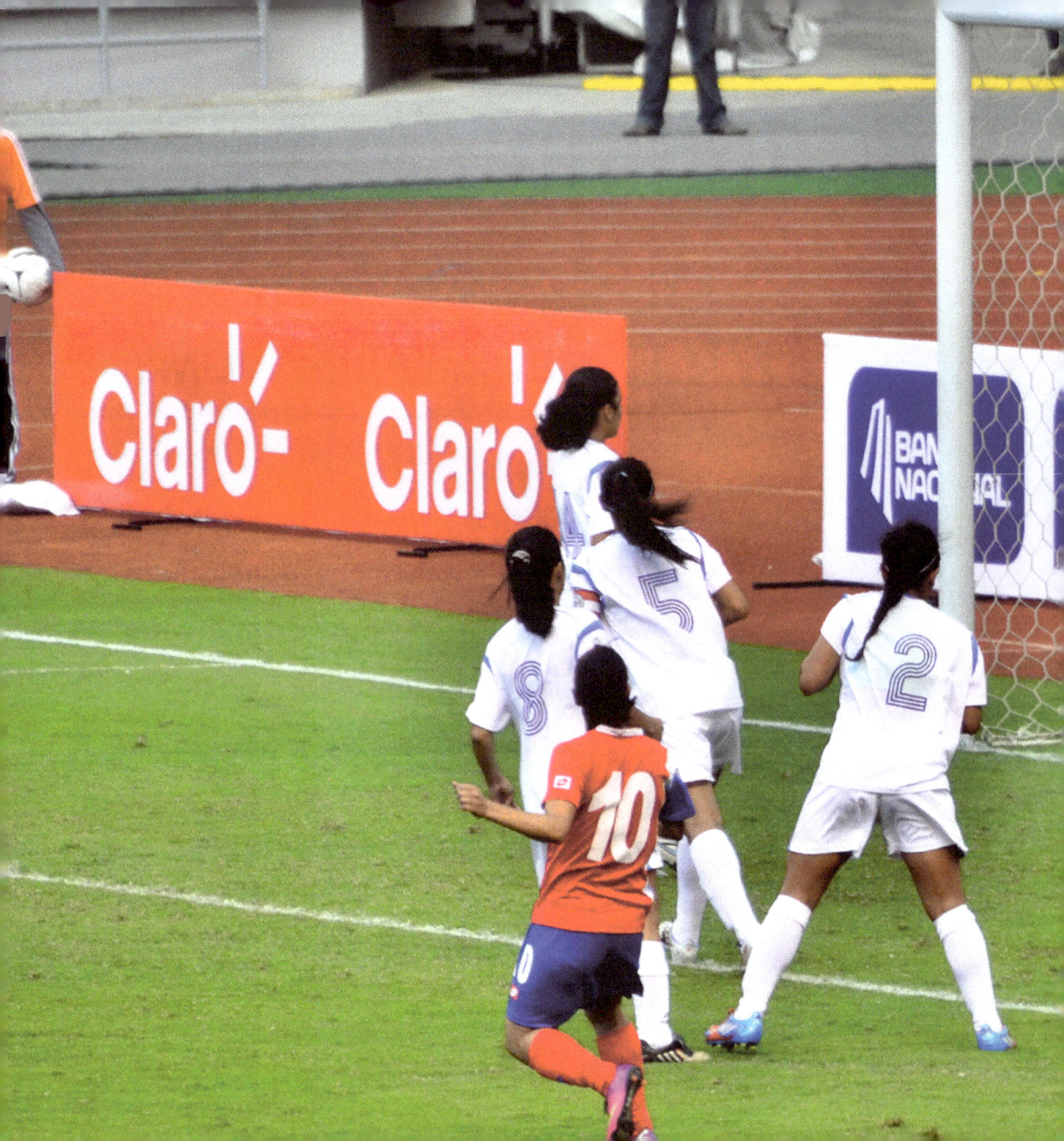

Claro
Claro

Read about other remarkable women in Baby Professor books like Empress Wu: Breaking and Expanding China, Roman Women: Second to Men but Equally Important, and Moms Needed Bread – The Women's March on Versailles.

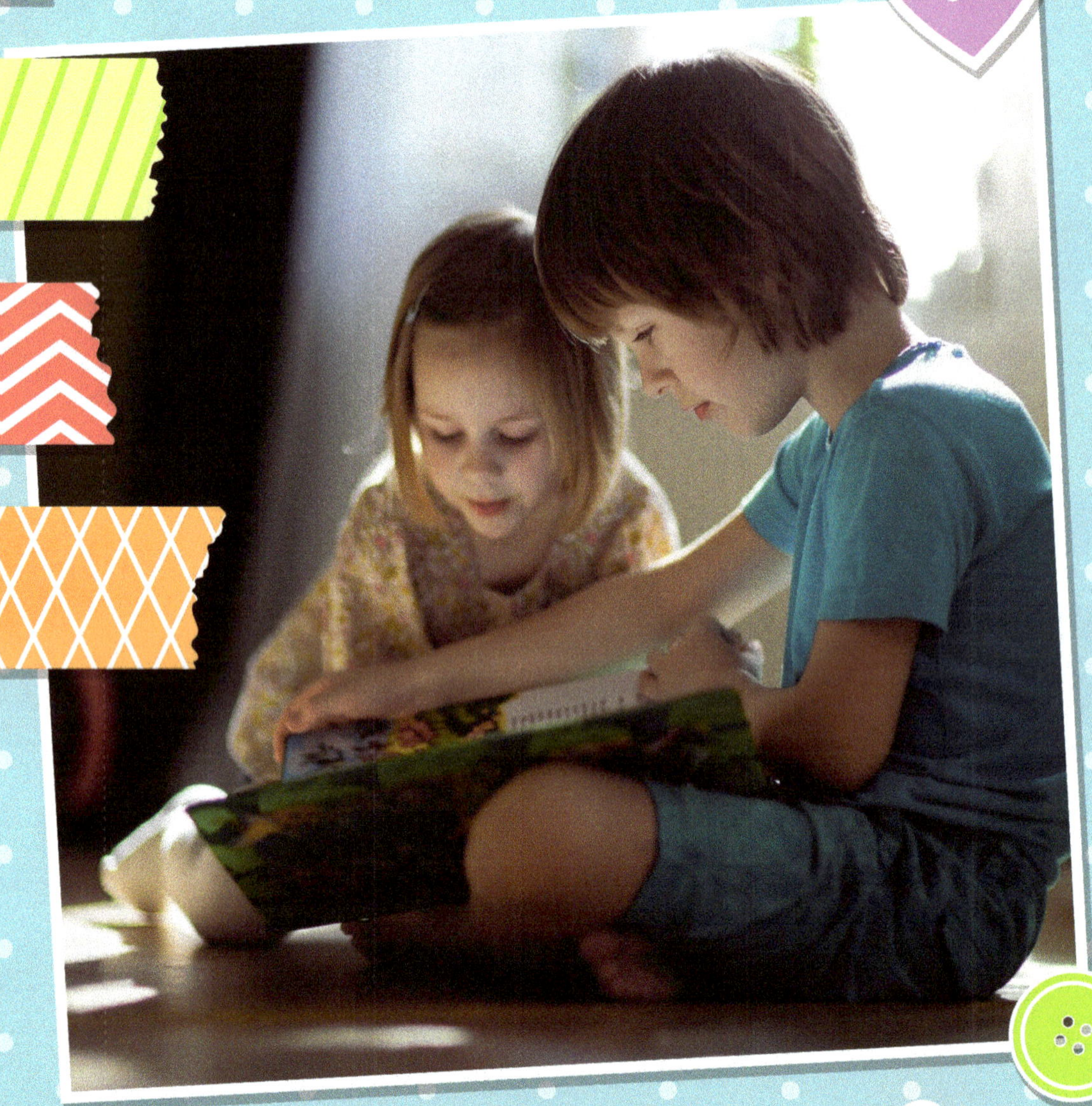

Visit

www.BabyProfessorBooks.com

to download Free Baby Professor eBooks and view our catalog of new and exciting Children's Books